HOW TO BE A VET

AND OTHER ANIMAL JOBS

WRITTEN BY
DR. JESS FRENCH

ILLUSTRATED BY
SOL LINERO

nosy crow

For my first love, Claws, the scruffy ginger cat
that inspired a lifetime of caring for animals
—J.F.

To the dogs of my life, Luna, Lobo,
Luca, Pecos, and Poncho
—S.L.

First published 2021 by Nosy Crow Ltd.
Wheat Wharf, 27a Shad Thames,
London, SE1 2XZ, UK

This edition published 2024 by Nosy Crow Inc.
145 Lincoln Road, Lincoln, MA 01773, USA

www.nosycrow.com

ISBN 979-8-88777-066-6

Nosy Crow and associated logos are trademarks
of Nosy Crow Ltd. Used under license.

Text © Dr. Jess French 2021
Illustrations © Sol Linero 2021

Library of Congress Catalog Card Number pending.

Printed in China.

Papers used by Nosy Crow are made from wood grown in sustainable forests.

10 9 8 7 6 5 4 3 2 1

CONTENTS

WHAT IS A VET?

Just like people, animals sometimes get sick. Vets, or veterinarians, are animal doctors that can help them to get better. Vets care for all sorts of different animals, from cats and hamsters to rhinos and flamingos.

Vets can be found all over the world. Some vets work in a **veterinary clinic.** This is a lot like a doctor's office. It is where we take our **pets** when they are **unwell.**

Other vets work with animals that are **too big** to bring to a clinic or hospital. Those vets must **travel** to see the animals where they live. Common places for a vet to visit are **farms, stables, and zoos.**

Vets sometimes work with **wild animals** too. These vets often have to travel a long way in difficult conditions to reach their patients.

Since pets can become unwell at **any time of day**, vets often **work long hours**, including overnight and on weekends.

Different vets need **different tools** to help them do their jobs. But there are some **basic things that all vets use:**

Gloves to stop the spread of disease

An **otoscope** to look in animals' ears

A **thermometer** to take an animal's temperature

A **stethoscope** to listen to an animal's heart and lungs

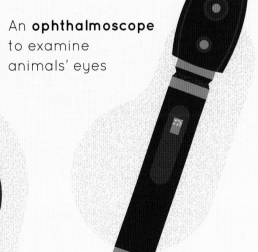

An **ophthalmoscope** to examine animals' eyes

A **calculator** to figure out how much medicine an animal needs

A **watch** to count how many times an animal's heart beats per minute

Using these tools, the vet's job is to **find out what is wrong** with their patient and to try and do something to **make it better.**

HOW DO
VETS HELP ANIMALS?

Being a vet is a bit like being a detective. When animals are sick or injured, they can't tell you how they are feeling or what hurts, so the vet's first job is to figure out what's wrong.

Making a diagnosis can take a very long time and may require **lots of equipment.**

Vets also spend time **talking to owners.** By asking the right questions, they can find out information that may be very important in solving the problem.

Once the diagnosis is determined, the vet's next job is to **fix the problem!** Some can be fixed by giving the animal **medicine.** Others need to be fixed by performing **surgery.**

Vets also work hard to stop animals from getting sick in the first place. They perform **check-ups,** or **wellness exams,** so they can spot problems early. They also give pets **vaccinations.** These are injections that teach animals' bodies how to fight off infection and disease.

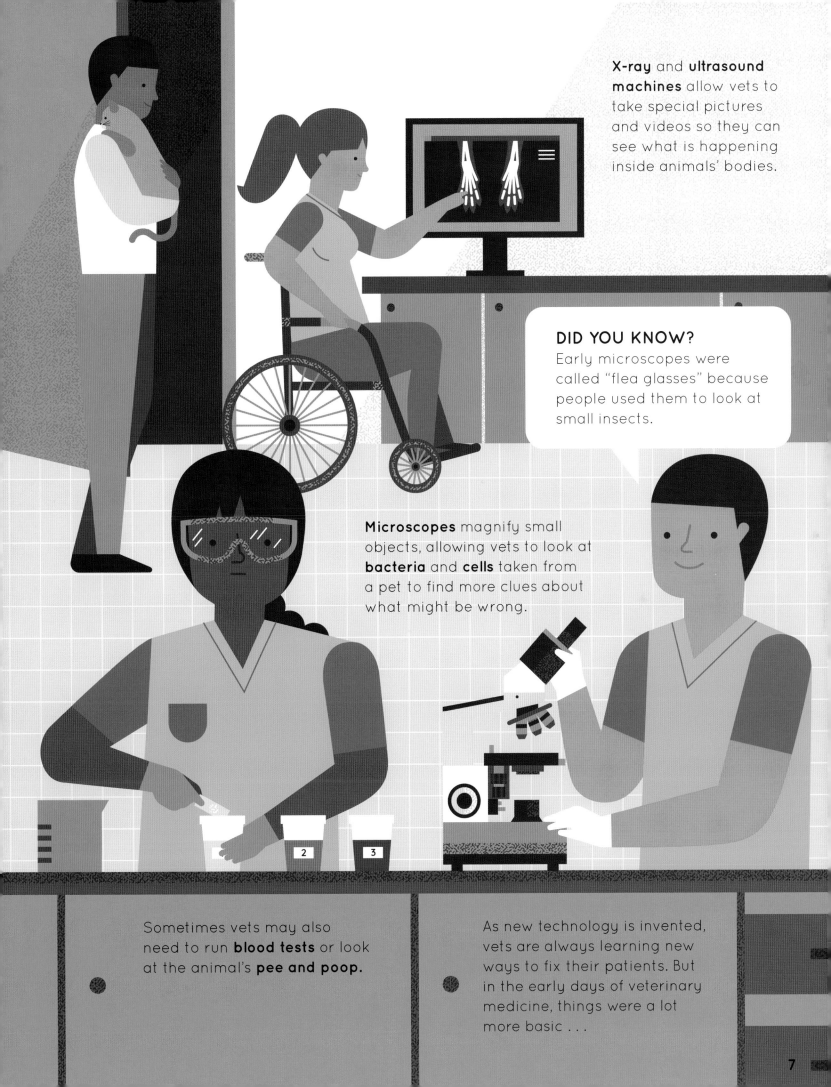

X-ray and **ultrasound machines** allow vets to take special pictures and videos so they can see what is happening inside animals' bodies.

DID YOU KNOW?
Early microscopes were called "flea glasses" because people used them to look at small insects.

Microscopes magnify small objects, allowing vets to look at **bacteria** and **cells** taken from a pet to find more clues about what might be wrong.

Sometimes vets may also need to run **blood tests** or look at the animal's **pee and poop.**

As new technology is invented, vets are always learning new ways to fix their patients. But in the early days of veterinary medicine, things were a lot more basic . . .

THE HISTORY OF
VETERINARY MEDICINE

Humans have kept animals for thousands of years. For as long as we have lived with animals, people have been interested in healing them when they are sick.

The first recorded vet was Urlugaledinna. He lived in an ancient civilization in the Middle East called Mesopotamia.

The first ever veterinary hospital was built by King Ashoka, an Indian emperor.

The first vaccinations were made for cattle following several disease outbreaks.

| 3000 BC | 500–300 BC | 265–238 BC | 1300s | 1712 | 1761 |

Greek philosophers like Aristotle and Alcmaeon studied animals to find out more about them.

The focus of veterinary medicine was on horses, which were used in war and transport. Most of their healing was done by **farriers,** who made and fitted horseshoes.

The world's first ever veterinary school was opened in Lyon, France. It focused on horses, sheep, and cattle.

Cats and dogs were becoming more popular as pets, so some vets started to specialize in treating smaller animals.

Many pets were abandoned during World War II. In England, a vet called Buster Lloyd Jones cared for many of them in his own home.

A vet named Louis J. Camuti became the first vet to work only with cats.

| 1900s | 1922 | 1939–1945 | 1960s | 1980s | 1990s |

Aleen Cust was the first woman to be recognized as a vet by the Royal College of Veterinary Surgeons.

DID YOU KNOW?
Fifty years ago, most vets were men. But now more than half of vets are women.

Drug companies started to produce lots of new animal medicines.

Veterinary practices continued to become more common in cities and suburbs, as pet ownership increased dramatically.

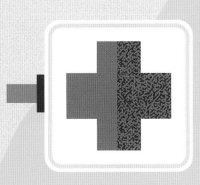

HOW DO YOU
BECOME A VET?

To become a vet, you must be patient, kind, and interested in solving problems. You also need to be good at **managing your emotions** because being a vet can sometimes be sad. It can be very upsetting when we have to say goodbye to very old or unwell animals. Luckily, vets are usually part of a friendly, caring team, so there are lots of kind people to talk to if you feel upset.

If you are interested in becoming a vet then you probably love animals, so you will really enjoy the first step—**spending lots of time with them!** There are many ways you can get experience working with animals:

Volunteer to walk dogs at a local dog shelter

Take care of your own **pets**

Help out with **milking** at a dairy farm

Help out with **grooming** at a local stable

Visit a sheep farm at **lambing** time, when baby lambs are born

DID YOU KNOW?
Most vets have completed at least 10 weeks of work experience with animals before even starting their veterinary training.

So, you love animals, solving problems, and are good at talking and listening to people? You have all the right skills to become a vet! But there is a lot of **training** to do first . . .

WHAT DO VETS NEED TO LEARN?

It takes a lot of studying to become a vet. First you must go to college and get a degree in animal science, biology, or a related area of study. Then you need to attend veterinary school, usually for an additional four years! There are not many veterinary schools and they are difficult to get into, so it is important that you work hard in school.

The most important subjects are **biology, chemistry, and math.** Chemistry will help you to understand how medicines work. Biology will teach you how animals' bodies work. Math will help you to calculate how much medicine to give to your patients.

The first years of study are all about learning **how animals' bodies work.** Young vets learn how every different system of the body works together to keep an animal healthy. There is a lot of **information to remember** and time spent **listening to experts** talk. But there are also **real animals** to meet!

DID YOU KNOW?
A dog's body contains around 350 pairs of muscles, each with a different name. That's a lot of new words to learn!

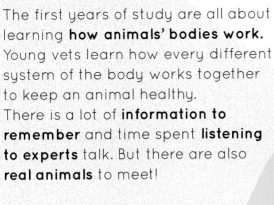

In the final year of vet school, students complete clinical rotations, where they gain hands-on experience. Students learn about different **medicines** and practice how to stitch up wounds and take blood. They **examine inside animals' bodies** with X-rays and ultrasounds.

They also look inside the bodies of animals that have died, to learn where all the organs are supposed to go. Finally, they learn how to **talk to owners** about their animals in a kind and friendly way.

After many years of training, it's time to decide which sort of vet you would like to be . . .

WHAT DO
SMALL ANIMAL VETS DO?

Small animal vets primarily look after **pets,** such as dogs, cats, rabbits, guinea pigs, hamsters, and even the odd bird! They must be good at **talking to owners** and **reassuring them** when their pets are unwell.

In the **reception or waiting area,** owners wait for their animals to be seen.

Getting a pet is a huge decision. Sometimes people will ask for a vet's **advice** about the best animal to join their family. Once their new pet arrives, most families will take it to see the vet.

On the first visit, the vet will check the pet from nose to tail in the **consultation room.** They may insert an electronic **microchip** under the animal's skin with an identification number so the owner can be contacted if the pet is lost.

They may also give the pet some **vaccinations** to prevent it from getting certain diseases and weigh it to start a record of its growth.

Any **medication** the pet needs, such as flea and deworming treatment, will be picked up later from the **pharmacy.**

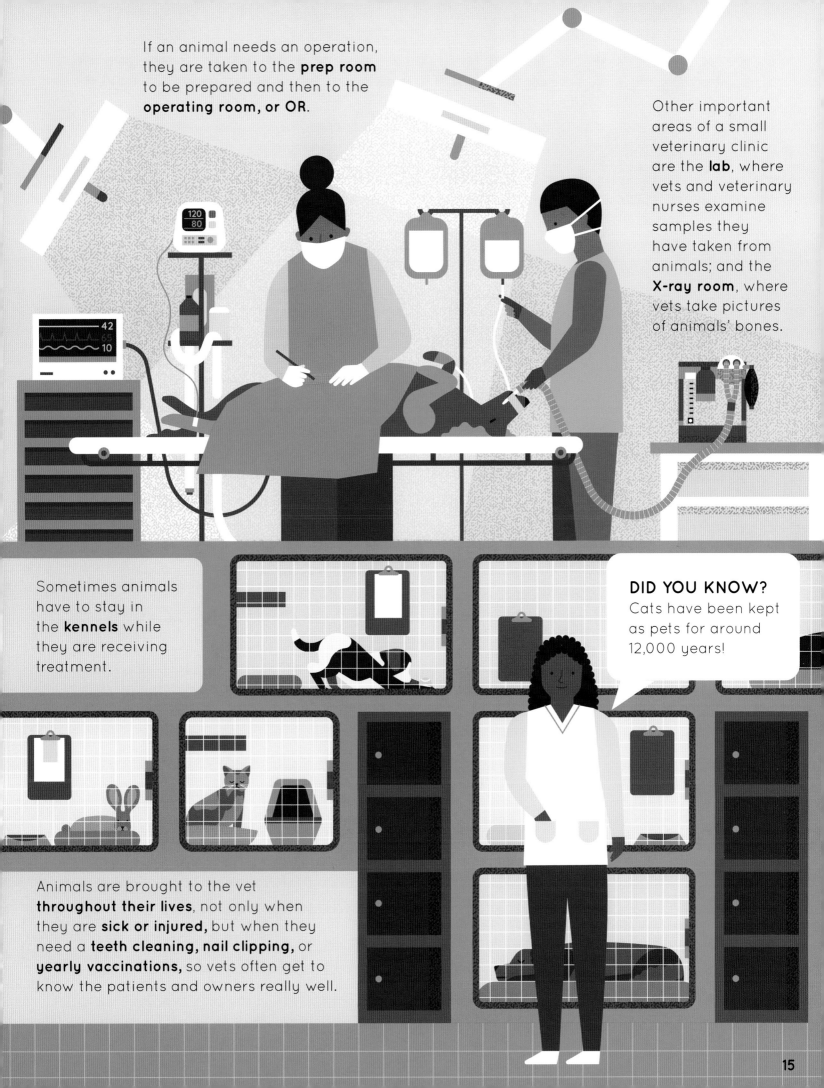

If an animal needs an operation, they are taken to the **prep room** to be prepared and then to the **operating room, or OR**.

Other important areas of a small veterinary clinic are the **lab**, where vets and veterinary nurses examine samples they have taken from animals; and the **X-ray room**, where vets take pictures of animals' bones.

Sometimes animals have to stay in the **kennels** while they are receiving treatment.

DID YOU KNOW?
Cats have been kept as pets for around 12,000 years!

Animals are brought to the vet **throughout their lives**, not only when they are **sick or injured,** but when they need a **teeth cleaning, nail clipping,** or **yearly vaccinations,** so vets often get to know the patients and owners really well.

WHAT DO
LARGE ANIMAL VETS DO?

There are two main types of vet that work with large animals. **Farm animal vets** work with sheep, pigs, goats, and cows, while **equine vets** work with horses and donkeys. Large animal vets usually have to drive around visiting their patients. They **work outside** in all kinds of weather and can end up very dirty!

Large animal vets have to do many jobs, from determining if cows are pregnant and delivering baby animals, to examining horses' feet and teeth.

They have to carry lots of important equipment in their car:

A **bucket** to wash in before doing surgery

A **portable X-ray machine** to take pictures of bones

A **surgical kit** to turn the stable or field into an operating theater

A **hoof pick** to clean animals' hooves

A **tooth rasp** to file down horses' teeth

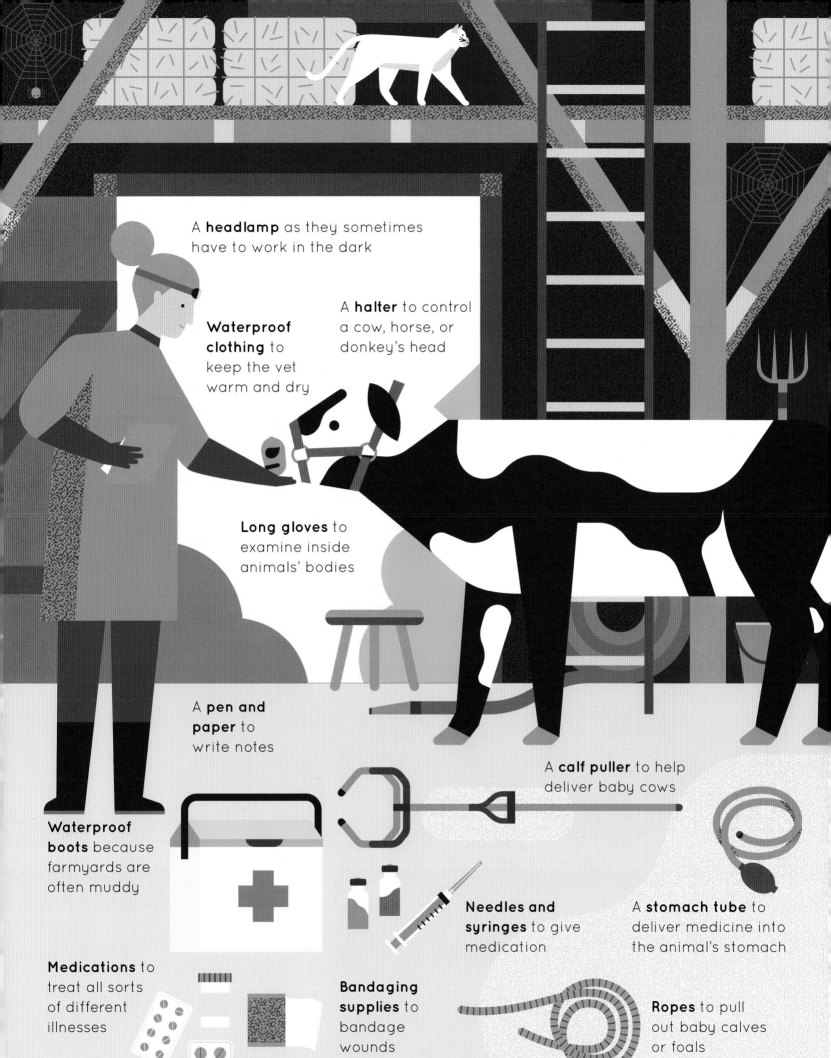

A **headlamp** as they sometimes have to work in the dark

Waterproof clothing to keep the vet warm and dry

A **halter** to control a cow, horse, or donkey's head

Long gloves to examine inside animals' bodies

A **pen and paper** to write notes

A **calf puller** to help deliver baby cows

Waterproof boots because farmyards are often muddy

Needles and syringes to give medication

A **stomach tube** to deliver medicine into the animal's stomach

Medications to treat all sorts of different illnesses

Bandaging supplies to bandage wounds

Ropes to pull out baby calves or foals

WHO TAKES CARE OF THE MORE
UNUSUAL ANIMALS?

Exotic vets work with animals like turtles, lizards, parrots, and snakes that are kept as pets. These creatures often need very particular conditions to survive. Providing these conditions is called **husbandry.** Exotic vets spend a lot of time teaching owners about the husbandry that will keep their pets healthy.

Seahorse

Turtle

Parrot

Lizard

Snake

Hedgehog

Axolotl

Zoo veterinarians work with animals that are **kept in wildlife parks and zoos**, from gorillas and lions to stick insects and tarantulas! Some zoos have their own vets, medications, and an operating room on site. Others have a vet that comes to visit when they need them.

Zoo vets need to know about all sorts of different animals and they are **constantly learning.** Some of the animals they care for are **dangerous** and must be sedated before the vet can look at them.

A typical day in the life of a zoo vet may include:

Checking new arrivals to the zoo to make sure they are healthy.

Giving vaccinations to prevent the animals from catching certain diseases.

Preparing animals that are leaving the zoo by doing blood tests and giving medication.

Sometimes a zoo animal might die and the vet will have to look inside their body, which is called a **post-mortem examination.** This is a sad job for the vet, but it is a good way to **learn more** about that type of animal and why it died.

Collecting poop samples, which is a great way to check the health of an animal without having to get too close.

DID YOU KNOW?
Zoo vets add colored lentils to their animals' food to help identify their poop!

VETS WORK?

If an animal's illness is particularly serious or complicated, they may be sent to a veterinary specialist. These vets are often experts in treating certain parts of the body.

Orthopedic surgeons fix broken bones.

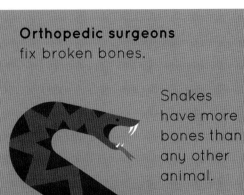

Snakes have more bones than any other animal.

Cardiologists are experts in hearts.

Squids have two hearts.

Ophthalmologists spend their time treating eyes.

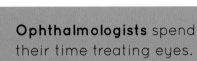

Bush babies have large eyes to see in the dark.

Dermatologists specialize in problems with the skin.

Frogs can breathe through their skin.

Neurologists know lots about the brain and nervous system.

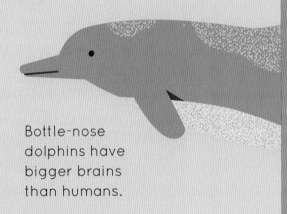

Bottle-nose dolphins have bigger brains than humans.

There are even **veterinary dentists** who work on animals' teeth.

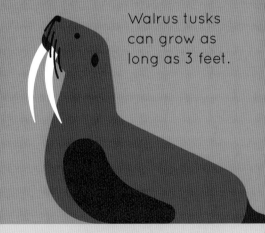

Walrus tusks can grow as long as 3 feet.

Vets can also specialize in working with a certain type of animal.

Poultry vets treat mainly chickens.

Camelid vets work with llamas and alpacas.

Avian vets specialize in treating birds.

Some vets work on **film sets**, where they make sure animals in films are treated well and stay healthy.

Sometimes vets have to do very upsetting jobs, such as visiting **slaughterhouses,** where animals are killed for meat. It is really important that vets visit these places to check that the animals are treated well before they are killed and that the meat is safe for people to eat.

Pet food companies employ vets to make sure their food is safe and nutritious.

Government vets help to make laws that protect animals and keep them safe.

Some vets work in **laboratories**, researching diseases and developing medicines that may save many animals' lives.

We also need vets at veterinary schools, **teaching** the vets of the future!

DID YOU KNOW?
The **military** employs vets to look after their dogs and horses. They must train as soldiers as well as completing their veterinary training.

Wherever they work, vets need the help of some very important people . . .

WHAT OTHER ANIMAL JOBS ARE THERE?

Vets could not do their jobs without many different people.
But what do these people actually do?

Groomers keep animals neat and clean. Sometimes they spot problems like dirty ears or broken nails that might be a sign of an illness, so they advise the owners to visit their vet.

DID YOU KNOW?
In Egyptian times, horseshoes were made out of animal skins, but now they are made of metal.

Behaviorists are specialists who understand animal behavior. If an animal is healthy but acting strangely, a behaviorist may be able to help.

Farriers are experts in horses' feet. They trim horses' hooves and make shoes to fit them properly.

Veterinary nurses are highly trained team members, who can give injections, take blood samples, help during operations, bandage wounds, and keep the clinic running smoothly. Most importantly, they specialize in giving the animals lots of love and cuddles.

Vets rely on **lab technicians** to perform tests on blood, pee, and poop to help them find the diagnosis and treat their patients.

Animal physical therapists work with vets to help animals that have problems getting around. From helping dogs to run on underwater treadmills to massaging horses' sore legs, their goal is to get their patients moving without pain.

DO YOU LIKE

KEEPING PEOPLE AND ANIMALS SAFE?

THEN ONE OF THESE JOBS MIGHT BE FOR YOU.

Many police departments use dogs to help them to solve crimes and keep people safe, and some officers, known as **mounted police,** patrol on horseback. **Specialized handlers** train and care for the animals that work in law enforcement.

Some dogs are specially bred to work as guide dogs, medical detection dogs, sniffer dogs, or therapy dogs. **Animal trainers** teach them the special skills they will need to succeed.

ASPCA workers investigate cases of animal cruelty and rescue animals that are being treated badly.

Sometimes wild animals need some love and special attention before they are released back into the wild. **Wildlife rehabilitators** nurse these creatures back to health so that they can be safely released.

Animal shelters provide safe places for animals that have had to leave their homes while they wait for a new family. **Animal care attendants** give them love and attention as well as cleaning, feeding, exercising, and playing with them.

People who need help walking or looking after their pets often rely on **dog walkers** and **pet sitters** to share the responsibility of caring for their animals.

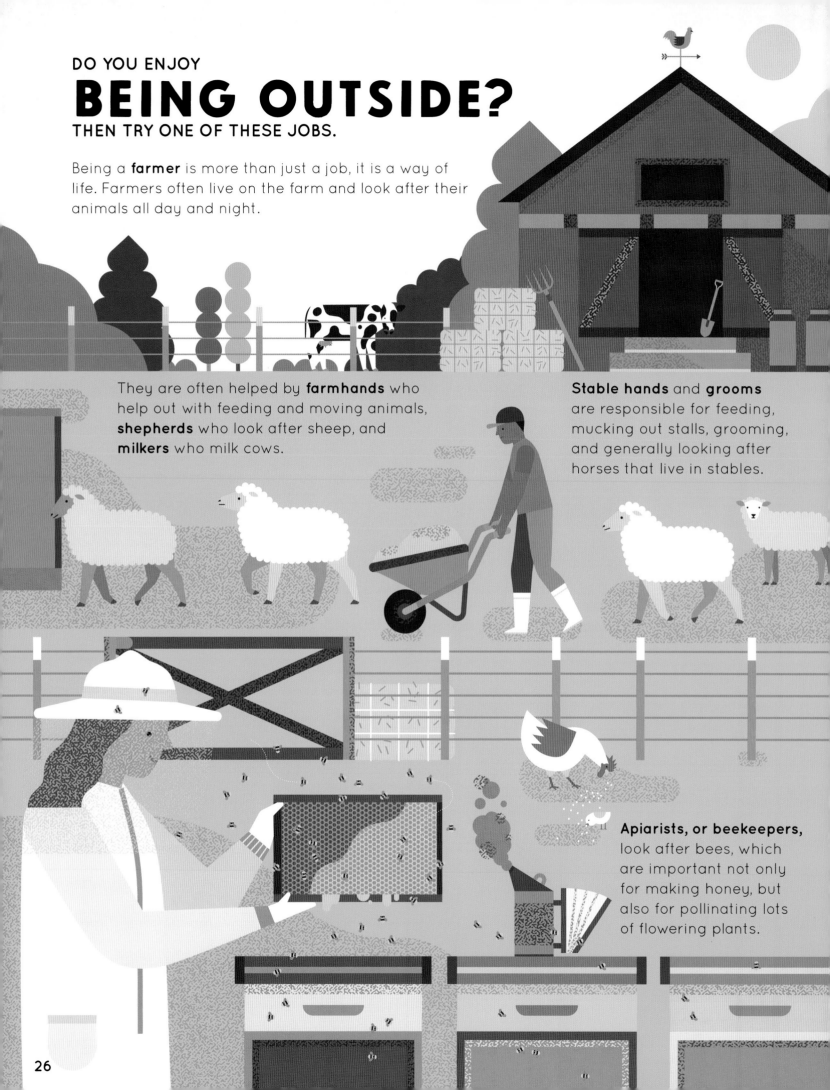

DO YOU ENJOY
BEING OUTSIDE?
THEN TRY ONE OF THESE JOBS.

Being a **farmer** is more than just a job, it is a way of life. Farmers often live on the farm and look after their animals all day and night.

They are often helped by **farmhands** who help out with feeding and moving animals, **shepherds** who look after sheep, and **milkers** who milk cows.

Stable hands and **grooms** are responsible for feeding, mucking out stalls, grooming, and generally looking after horses that live in stables.

Apiarists, or beekeepers, look after bees, which are important not only for making honey, but also for pollinating lots of flowering plants.

Zoos often have a big team of **volunteers** that help out too.

Zookeepers take care of animals that are housed in zoos and wildlife parks. They usually specialize in one area, such as the aquarium or the reptile house.

Jockeys are the people who ride horses in races. They are usually very small and light.

Exercise riders ride horses between races to keep them fit. They can be taller and heavier than jockeys.

Riding instructors teach people how to ride horses.

Horse trainers teach horses how to behave and understand their riders' commands.

WHAT ABOUT WORKING WITH
ANIMALS IN THE WILD?

If you are most at home on a nature walk with a pair of binoculars and a notebook, then you would probably love one of these jobs working with wild animals.

Research scientists work "in the field," studying animals and their environments so that we can learn more about them.

Ichthyologists study fish, sharks, and rays.

Ornithologists specialize in birds.

Herpetologists are experts in amphibians and reptiles.

Primatologists work with primates like lemurs, monkeys, and even gorillas and chimpanzees.

Entomologists study insects.

Camera operators and **photographers** can spend months watching animals in the wild, waiting to capture the perfect moment on film.

Conservation programs, which protect endangered animals, need **vets, zoologists,** and **volunteers** to care for animals in rescue centers and to help release animals back into the wild.

Nature guides take people on trips into incredible wild spaces and tell them about the animals that live there.

In countries where poaching is a big problem, **anti-poaching rangers** protect animals from being killed by illegal hunters.

Conservation officers and **park rangers** look after wild areas and make sure they are cared for properly.

Dive masters take people scuba diving to see the amazing creatures that live under the sea.

WHAT ABOUT THE MORE
UNUSUAL ANIMAL JOBS?

If you love animals and the environment and want to share your passion with lots of other people, then maybe you could become a **writer** or **television researcher.**

You could explain recent scientific discoveries, show well-known behaviors in new and exciting ways, or even describe a brand-new species!

Snake venom is sometimes used to make human medicines. Specially trained zoologists, called **snake milkers,** know how to get this venom from snakes safely and without hurting them.

Animal nonprofit groups do wonderful work, from protecting endangered habitats to saving pets from homes where they are being mistreated. But without enough money, these organizations would not be able to function. **Fundraisers** have the difficult job of raising money for these groups so that they can continue their good work.

TFB **THE FIRST BANK**

Date September 25

Pay to the order of ___Animals Foundation___ **$ 5,000**

Five thousand and 00/100 _____ Dollars

For ___Rescue equipment___   Signature _____

Bug wranglers are experts in insects and arachnids. They work with film and television producers who need bugs to perform specific movements and behaviors.

Pathologists are interested in what causes diseases. They examine animals' bodies after they have died to see if they can find out what made them sick. They are often involved in the creation of new medicines that can save many animals' lives.

When animals are kept in captivity, it is important to make their surroundings look similar to their natural habitat. A **zoo designer's** job is to create spaces that make zoo animals feel totally at home.

GET INVOLVED!

If you would like to learn more about becoming a vet or working with animals,
there are many things you can do . . .

You can get in touch with a local animal nonprofit or rescue,
join a local nature-watching group, or even start your own
club to learn about and care for the animals in your area.

All you need to get started is a passion and a love for
all animals and the world they live in.

ORGANIZATIONS AND WEBSITES TO EXPLORE:

Vet Set Go www.vetsetgo.com
ASPCA www.aspca.org
NatGeo Kids kids.nationalgeographic.com
World Wildlife Fund www.worldwildlife.org